Showdown on da Muddy Banks

A Tale of Right Down, Rippin' Radical, River Rat Resolve

Told by

Richard "Dickie" Dempsey

Illustrated by Najla Kay

SCAN FOR AUDIO

Showdown on da Muddy Banks
A Tale of Right Down, Rippin' Radical, River Rat Resolve

Published by Richard C. Dempsey, Lakeland, FL

Copyright © 2025 *by Richard C. Dempsey*

Interior Illustrations by Najla Kay

Cover Design by Theddee Rheyshelle

ISBN: (hardcover)

ISBN: (paperback)

Printed in the United States of America

Dear Reader...

This true-life parable of mine is meant to transport you back to a much simpler time when summers seemed to last forever, kids were free to roam from morning until long after dark, fireflies filled the night air, and all the heavenly lights were so much brighter. It was a different world back then. Parents were less fearful and not as overly concerned about where we went or what we were doing. At noon, a city-wide siren would sound, and we'd all head home for a quick bite before making a mad dash back outside for more adventure.

In keeping with yesteryear's laid-back way of life, this tale is told in the dawdling, unhurried vernacular of the folk who lived on the river. My recommendation is that you grab something to drink, settle into a comfortable chair, take a few deep breaths, and slooowwww waaay down. If not, you just might miss the entire experience; and the *right down, rippin' radical* message I've come to deliver.

From this page forward, it's you, me, and the boys who lived on the muddy banks of the Passaic that one hot, muggy, memorable summer day in 1956... a day that forevermore changed my attitude toward the roadblocks and pitfalls of life.

Richard "Dickie" Dempsey

Introduction
The River

The beginnin's of my life were spent playin', explorin' and, in general, lookin' fer adventure on the muddy banks of the river that wound its way through the northern edge of our town. This was a time b'fore environmentalists clamped down on the various industries, ya know, them ones what routinely got rid of all manner of toxic chemicals in the most convenient place: the river.

These industrial contributions gave the river a dynamic ability to change hues from day to day dependin' on what was bein' manufactured upstream. Ya jist never knowed what color she'd be a wearin'. Whilst her most worn shade 'twere a mundane, murky, greenish brown, I've seen that river run as red as the bloody Nile, blue as a Jay's tail feathers, and, on occasion, a luminous slime green as bright as the eighteenth hole on a putt-putt golf course. The buoyant consistency of this colorful water was not unlike the Dead Sea in its ability to support the floatin' islands, of mysterious dusky foam, lazily makin' their way on the gentle current that would take them to the Big Apple and, eventually, into the not-so-blue Atlantic. Another easily identifiable feature of the river was her delicate perfume—the smell of decay and mud and chemicals which evermore hung about the ol' gal.

In hindsight, I can't imagine lettin' my kids loose to be a playin' unattended on the banks of the river as it was offen a dangerous place, whether it be high and rushin' or done froze over. Why, even my brother accidently broke through the ice one day and found hisself fightin' fer his life—one of the scads of thangs my momma weren't never told. In addition, it were at the river that I seen all manner of mayhem and mischief folk do when they be a thinkin' ain't nobody a watchin'. Yet with all these hazards and perils, the river was a favorite place of mine to play and explore.

'Twas on the banks of this river, up on log stilts, that the Oblonski family made their home, occupyin' that two-story shack throughout my childhood. Whilst missin' all the modern-day gadgets enjoyed by most at the time, that ol' place come with a unique way of simplifyin' ev'ry household's most mundane task: takin' out the trash. From a handy trap door in the kitchen floor, they dropped their unwanted scraps to the ground below to await foragin' beasts or high water—a one-of-a-kind flushin' system that the greedy currents of the river seemed to relish and performed with some degree of regularity.

Bubba n' Junior were my contemporaries. However, I must admit I never felt quite at ease bein' in their immediate proximity. What I can't explain is... I was on hand fer some purdy precarious happenin's—although in my mind never as a participant, but rather as an impartial observer and eager student. I guess, like the chameleon my pa bought my brother and me at the Ringlin' Brothers, Barnum and Bailey Circus, I musta had the uncanny ability to safely blend in with my surroundin's; cuz my mem'ry bares evidence that, as a young lad, I was privy to some of the most awe-inspirin' messiness humankind had to offer at that time.

Thinkin' back, I must notta had a lick a sense or the brains God gave a chimpanzee to be forevermore a puttin' myself in harm's way. I jist remember the river bein' a place of fun and adventure, as well as a source of great entertainment. Sorta like Roy Rogers, Hop Along Cassidy, Red Rider, Dick Tracy, and whatever else a set of rabbit ears would yield on the seven-inch, black and white television my family sometimes gathered 'round to watch.

I reckon I've always found unusual folk to be interestin'. The more bizarre they are, the more fascinated I become—ya know, like starin' at that little television a fearin' if I blinked I's gonna miss sumthin'. And let me tell ya, the folk on the river, well, 'tweren't nuttin ordinary 'bout them 'tall. As far as I's concerned, they seem to have been placed on earth to entertain the rest of us less gifted folk, introducin' us to the endless possibilities of our baser natures, and grantin' us the rights to the passin' on of their heritage and folklore—of the which I have taken much advantage over the years.

I must admit, I have been accused, on occasion, of makin' up some of these stories; but iffen ya have any notion to that end, I will tell ya right cheer and right now, this one is true to the best of my knowledge and belief. Cross my heart. I have changed the names to protect the guilty. With that bein' said, it sorta explains why most of my Bubba n' Junior tales start with the words, "Y'all ain't gonna believe this, but…"

CHAPTER 1
Bubba n' Junior

Y'all ain't gonna believe this, but… one hot, muggy summer day, I was a sittin' on the rotted wooden steps that led up and into the home shared by the Oblonski family jist a watchin' Bubba n' Junior, their two youngest. Them yahoos were attemptin' to extricate gasoline from a dump truck belongin' to Uncle Jerry—one of the "uncles" currently abidin' with their older sisters, and therefore 'mediately achievin' the coveted status of a legit Oblonski relative, however short-term.

Bubba was on his knees in the dust of the dirt driveway with a rusty, dented, faded yeller and red gas can and a piece of tattered, avocada-green, garden hose 'bout four feet long. One end of the hose had been carefully snaked into the filler tube of Uncle Jerry's gas tank, and the other end was currently, that's right, in Bubba's mouth.

I must point out here that both Bubba n' Junior had skills at their age that the rest of the kid-population did not possess. They were at this juncture, as I was, somewheres betwixt the age of eight and ten. Bubba, a year older than Junior, was takin' the lead in this particular daylight raid on Uncle Jerry's dump truck.

This, I later came to realize, was jist a small portion of a much more sophisticated and diabolical plan complete with—what I've since learned to be—extreme malice of forethought.

This current phase of the plan tweren't goin' well 'tall. After endurin' several mouthfuls of Uncle Jerry's gasoline, Bubba was a recitin' all the words the rest of us youngsters didn't dare utter. Every time Bubba got a mouth full of petrol, he would take to cussin' and a spittin' it out as he moved the hose quickly from his mouth to the mouth of the red and yeller gas can. Then losin' his flow, he'd cuss a nuther blue streak, returnin' the hose to his mouth as iffen it was drier than the desert and desperate fr anythang wet. Bubba finally managed to get enough of the gasoline out of Uncle Jerry's dump truck and into the waitin' can… not to mention, all over the can, the hose, the ground and, more or less, on hisself.

This process woulda been highly entertainin' in its own right; however, what made it an even more magnetic performance—to which my eyes were glued—was the fact that Junior was a standin' a short ways off, dancin' 'round and flickin' lit matches in high arcs which were terminatin', yes indeedy, in Bubba's personal space.

Seemin'ly enraptured with his pursuit, Junior's eyes followed each flamin' projectile as it climbed to its apex. Then, based on a thousand insignificant variables—like wind current, phosphorous content of the individual match, matchbook history, thumb pressure, angle and velocity of delivery, biometric pressure and humidity factors—it done extinguished itself leavin' a trail of smoke, mostly landin' harmlessly, like I said, in Bubba's personal space.

Bubba, fiercely intent with his hose-suckin' project, did not seem to notice this current sportin' event to which his younger brother was a participatin'. Both boys jist seemed to be doin' their appointed task fer the day without a shadow of a question as to why or what might be the sure-fire end of such a practice.

As most of y'all know, there are twenty paper matches in the traditional give-away matchbook that would come a bouncin' down into the lower tray of the cigrette vendin' machines that use ta be a sittin' everywheres, back then, accompanied by the thirty-five-cent purchase of Camels, Pall Malls, Lucky Strikes or Chesterfields. These matchbooks were similar in most ways; and, whilst included as a means of lightin' them thar smokes, they offen wound up in the grubby hands of enterprisin' young lads like meself. With the post war advent of the Zippo, them matches tended to be left in the tray, lendin' them to be easy access to our God-given curiosity 'bout thangs like campfires, firearms, firecrackers and other potentially destructive forces, of the which, but nonetheless, were desperately desired. Matchbooks were, in that phase of life, the only item on the list that was quite readily available to rovin' eight-year-olds in search of adventure.

At the time, I suspect I thought flickin' matches were an excitin' and reasonable practice, not knowin' much about the characteristics of accelerants. Lookin' back at Junior's delight whilst he was a flickin' them thar matches, I'm thinkin' he knew a lot more than I did. Bottom line, I don't recall objectin'—not that I was brave enough to object to anythang one of them hoodlums was up to. Although Junior was genuinely enjoyin' hisself, not much seemed to be happenin'. Knowin' the limited number of matches in a matchbook, I was jist a watchin' and a waitin' fer him to run out, figgerin' that would be game over. I done figgered wrong.

And now, as much as I hate to, I hafta leave this scene with a blazin' phosphorous projectile suspended in mid-flight, the thick, sultry summer air a reekin' of gasoline, river scum, and the familiar smell of burnin' matches to explain the nefarious beginnin's of the entire petrol-stealin' operation and the evil plot that was to foller.

CHAPTER 2
Culture and Setting

Ya see, folk who lived on the river—most commonly known as *river rats*—could be a tad bit odd, especially when compared to the general population. I don't rightly know iffen it was the river water or the aforementioned toxic fumes a driftin' up from the surface that may have affected their personalities and dispositions so adversely, but in all the ways that you and I might consider to be *normal*, the kids on the river were "jist plain differ'nt."

Fer one thang, although consistently grimier, they seemed to be a heck of a lot more inventive and resourceful, as well as a tad bit more savvy than the neighborhood boys I played baseball with. They were gifted with an alien and, in some respects, far superior intelligence than I possessed at that age. And, fer some strange reason, they did not need to be a sittin' in borin' classrooms listenin' to the benefits of long division like the rest of us; and nobody seemed to bother them none too much about it. Fer us non-privileged and imprisoned students, we thought these kids was jist plain lucky.

Despite what appeared to me to be, a meager existence, they were quite pleased and content with their lifestyle. One might even say, they were "river rat" proud. They had their own culture, were governed by a whole nuther set of rules, and lived unburdened by the thoughts of tomorrow. As far as they's concerned, they'd already done arrived. They had it all. *What more could a body want or need?*

Whilst us kids on La Secla Place lived on the first street off the river and was only separated by several acres of, what we called, "the woods," we was not as fortunate in our thinkin'. The Sears and Roebuck Christmas Catalogue and Sunday Night Disney TV had us all a wishin' and a wantin' fer *more*. We yearned fer the day when we could walk through those sacred gates of Disneyland. Why, this was the unreachable dream of every kid on the east coast with a television. At least them ones what I knew.

As a child, our home seemed to be worlds away from that of Bubba n' Junior's; even though at certain times, iffen the wind were right, we shared in such benefits the river provided as the heavy smell of mud, dead fish and chemicals wafted its way up the hill and emanated from the woods behind our home. As I saw it, the woods was the divide what made the fundamental differ'nce 'tween river rats and us less entertainin', run-of-the-mill kids on La Secla Place.

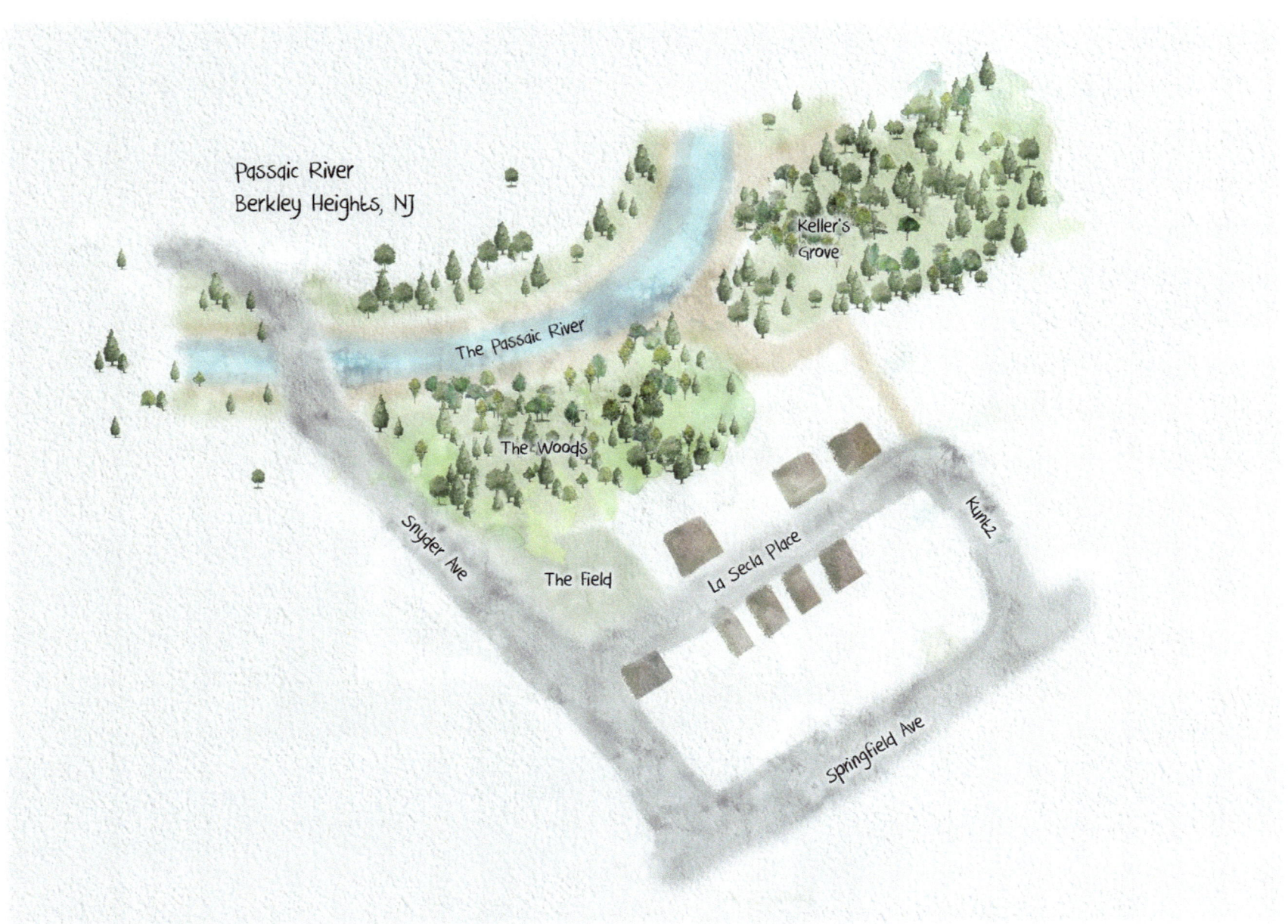

Passaic River
Berkley Heights, NJ

Keller's Grove

The Passaic River

The Woods

Snyder Ave

The Field

La Secla Place

Kuntz

Springfield Ave

The majority of the boys on the block had only fleetin' and careful contact with Bubba n' Junior, as those two were notorious "dirty fighters" and as unpredictable as hungry gators. Any contact they did have was mostly fer some manner of inevitable warfare consistin' of dirt clods and rocks. I guess I was a peaceful sort, skillfully a ridin' the cultural fence, attemptin' to get along with the area diversity, and therefore, avoidin' the pervasive beatin's which river rats, Italians, and other surly youngsters roamin' the area were known to dish out jist fer fun—even within my tender age group. Afterall, a scrawny kid like me had to know his limitations and exercise all the wisdom accessible to him. Consequently, I was "diverse" before "diverse" existed. But pay me no never mind. This ol' man's done taken to ramblin'.

In the 50's, my hometown was made up of second-generation, European immigrants who tended to cluster together by country of origin, each and all considerin' themselves to be a tad bit superior to those from the less cool, and obviously inferior, nations. We all resided in, what was historically known as, "Turkey Town," founded by, governed by, policed by, and dominated by Italians.

As fate would have it, my parents descended from a differ'nt and—no doubt, in my pa's estimation, of course—a far superior country called Ireland. This offen proved a tad bit awkward in a town predominantly made up of Italians; but thank the good Lord, we was all Catholics. 'Twas our family's savin' grace, in the name of the Father, and of the Son, and of the Holy Ghost, amen.

Bubba 'n Junior, accordin' to my pa, were Polish and, although most prob'ly Catholic, they did not attend the Church of Our Lady of Eternal Sorrow like the rest of us kids—renderin' themselves obviously "less than" and not quite good enough to hang around with, much less deemed worthy of any sort of camaraderie.

Furthermore, they did not share in the sufferin' through endless Catechism lessons under the evil eye of Sister Mary Louise. This led those of us sharin' this common bond of mis'ry—spendin' school recesses and summer vacations in the basement of the church—to only one possible conclusion: river rats (and Bubba n' Junior in particular) were either the luckiest boys in the county or the actual spawn of Satan.

19

Back then, in the absence of the more obvious racial differ'nces based on skin color, human profilin' was a more subtle art, seein' that this entire town were made up of white folk. Nonetheless, we always managed to find someone a rung b'low us fer any eclectic reason our pa might invent. Even Bubba n' Junior seemed to share in this dim view of equality amongst all men. That said, they managed to find someone a rung or two b'low them, namely, in the personage of Little Davy Hendrickson.

The mere existence of this small, skinny, and (strangely enough) grimier kid offered Bubba n' Junior momentary reprieves from bein' looked down upon and provided them with a ready-made means to experience the power and superiority they seemed to so earnestly desire.

No doubt it was this "food chain mentality" that added to the complex river rat syndrome and overall contrary natures and paradoxical values of a Bubba n' Junior—especially when it came to the likes of Little Davy. I'm purdy darn sure that none of us civilized folk would engage in such debauched thinkin' in today's progressive atmosphere, but pay this old man no never mind. It seems I've done taken to ramblin' again.

Chapter 3
Little Davy

Whilst the Oblonksi boys both awed and frightened me, I found Davy to be a strange but friendly sort. In fact, I kinda liked him. Fer one thang, bein' the smallest and scrawniest kid in the neighborhood, I's quite pleased to be in the company of one even smaller and scrawnier than I was. As a little half-breed Cherokee and a Protestant of some sort to boot, this raggamuffin had two strikes agin' him before he even done left the house. As fer me, I've always been a sucker fer the underdog.

Davy was the only offspring of the caretaker of the local Beer Garden and a grassy picnic area known as Keller's Grove. I don't specifically know what Keller's Grove was all about, other than bein' at the dead end of a dirt road and a teeterin' on the banks of an obviously very polluted river. It was the site of a few small, annual company picnics and a mid-summer Purina Dog Show that an inventive kid could easily enter by scoutin' out a ticket discarded by an actual payin' participant. It was a won'erful source of hot dogs and soda—not that I knowed this from any personal experience, mind ya.

Little Davy, on account of his pa, had the run of it all… the bar, the shed behind it, and the mysterious Grove. He loved to play "tour guide" and would proudly and ceremoniously show me 'round, hands tucked in his overalls, a rockin' back and forth on his muddy bare feet, and a pointin' out all the secret nooks and crannies of Keller's Grove. Invariably this tour culminated in the latest version of his diverse and beloved collection of dead animals in various stages of decomposition, the likes of which he kept carefully lined up in rows out behind the tool shed by the banks of the river.

With its ample crop of these dead creatures floatin' in the debris on the surface, caught in eddies, or tangled in dead brush along the muddy banks, the river was, of course, the most obvious resource fer the diligent pursuit of his downright unusual hobby. Therefore, it behooved Davy to have a watercraft of some sort by which to feed his eight-year-old passion. Ya may not believe this, but that lil' urchin took to buildin' hisself a boat usin' a screen door and a bunch of raincoats he had somehow acquired—undoubtedly from the "lost and found" box in the shed behind the Beer Garden at Keller's Grove.

Little Davy commenced to stitchin' the raincoats together with fishin' line and daubin' the seams with roofin' cement from his daddy's shed. To my utter awe, that thirty-pound-soakin'-wet-whippersnapper of a kid was able to make his homemade boat honest-to-God float—further proof of the exaggerated ingenuity of this youngster and the fundamental truth behind necessity and an absolute lack of resources bein' the mother of such inventions.

The mere existence of this watercraft, however, is what done shoved Bubba n' Junior's feverish disdain fer Davy over the edge into a pure, unadulterated, envy-fueled, white-hot hatred. Ya see, Bubba n' Junior had a record of several failed attempts at tryin' to build a boat or steal a boat—one of them bein' from my own driveway.

Imagine my pa's dismay when he looked out the livin' room window to see Bubba n' Junior abscondin' with a kayak he had borrowed fer our weekend trip to the lake. Serge, the older neighbor boy across the street, had done built it; and now here was Bubba n' Junior just a draggin' and a pullin' that kayak down La Secla Place. My pa took to runnin' and a hollerin' after them, at which time them two would-be thieves dropped that kayak in the middle of the road and ran off fer the woods.

I'm comin' over to tell y'all, Bubba 'n Junior were desperate fer a boat; and thusly, jist could not tolerate the rank audacity of this dirty little river rat with a nasty hobby, single-handedly, buildin' hisself such a fine watercraft. Each time they seen him a paddlin' upstream to parts unknown and then later a cruisin' back down with the current of the river, they burned with hatred and took to hurlin' whatever makeshift ammo they could find, with little or no degree of success.

And so, it happened on that very warm, humid, bright summer mornin', Little Davy in his fine boat—consistin' of a screen door bent and twisted in the general shape of a makeshift dinghy covered in raincoats—made his way upstream usin' a broken-handled shovel fer a paddle. He almost, jist nearly, slipped right on past the watchful eyes of both Bubba n' Junior.

Upon becomin' alert to his silent progress paddlin' upstream, Bubba n' Junior tore down to the river's edge a slippin' and a slidin' in the mud, pickin' up rocks, bottles, and tin cans on their way, jist a cussin' and a swearin' 'bout the nerve of the boy not givin' them due notice as to this particular voyage. They commenced to tryin' to nail the little ship's captain with a barrage of their makeshift ammo, but Davy hugged the north bank while passin' their shack and there-wise easily escaped serious injury.

Needless to say, now madder than a couple of scalded dogs and feedin' themselves a steady diet of the greenest variety of boat-envy, the boys began to weave an evil scheme. Their plan involved acquirin' gasoline from Uncle Jerry's dump truck, a book of matches, a glass jug, a rag, rocks in the right caliber and configuration fer accurate throwin', a shovel, and a burial site. Additionally, included in this vile plot was an incidental and unofficial change of ownership of the aforementioned, one-of-kind, home-made watercraft.

This here, of course, takes us back to Bubba attemptin' his surreptitious daylight raid on Uncle Jerry's dump truck; and Junior jist a' flickin' them thar matches.

CHAPTER 4
The Plan

As you and I head back to me jist a sittin' on the rotted steps a watchin' these two varmints, the sound we're lookin' fer here is a *HU-WHOMP!* Turns out, this ain't a sound ya wanna hear in yer own front yard.

As the sinister plan fer the demise of Little Davy unfolded, one lone, maverick, paper matchstick come off Junior's thumb with a little more than its share of that red stuff on the end and jist enough of the right stuff innit to keep it goin' in spite of what might have been the aforementioned adverse atmospheric conditions. That flamin' match seemed to pause majestically in the air, and then ever so delicately continue, end over end, a small movn' flash on its way to a terrifyin' *HU-WHOMP!*

Mind ya, this here match was a' bein' flicked by Junior, who—havin' barely gone to school a day in his life— was still workin' on shoe-tyin' and a learnin' his letters by eatin' alphabet soup. I'm tellin' ya, that boy hadn't a lick of sense. And, apparently, all my three years of lower education hadn't done me much good neither, as what came next was a complete surprise.

The avocada-colored piece of garden hose where the match touched down was, of course, covered with gasoline; as was the yeller and red dented up can; as was the filler pipe comin' from the gas tank of Uncle Jerry's dump truck, as was Bubba. And before ya could say, "Jack Robinson," all of the aforementioned were enveloped in a spectacular, brilliant orange, *HU-WHOMPIN'* fireball. Son, I jist nearly jumped mile!

While Junior found the initial result here very funny and took to laughin' his li'l behind off, Bubba, bein' a bit more personally involved and at the epicenter of the *HU-WHOMP*, didn't seem the least bit amused. Not normally knowed fer speed, Bubba executed one jiffy of a "stop, drop and roll" without havin' had the previous benefit of instruction. Luckily, the ordinarily muddy drive did, at this stage of summer, contain some fine dust; and Bubba seemed to burrow into it like a mole in the crosshairs of a rat terrier.

From this spectator's perspective, all of this seemed to go down in slow-motion, engravin' ev'ry minute detail into my eight-year-old remembrances.

34

Junior, finally seein' Bubba in flames and all, was on him like a duck on a June bug. He went to a gufawin' and a beatin' out the flames with the soles of his lace-less, second-hand PF Flyers. It appeared that he had been taught, at some point, to "stomp" outta fire, even when the flames happened to be located on a person's body.

Once't the scant growth of blonde fuzz from Bubba's per-usual "skinned onion" haircut had sizzled off to blackened nubs, and his face and arms appeared to have been too darn long in the sun without the benefit of modern stuff like SPF 45; he simply looked at Junior through his now lash-less, reptilian eyes. There was a tense moment where one had to wonder iffen Bubba was fixin' to keel over… or kill Junior. He sat there in the dust jist a starin' at his brother with this here strange look on his blackened face.

Thinkin' back now, after watchin 'bout three billion automobile explosions on our seven inch, black and white television, Uncle Jerry's dump truck was ev'ry bit a disappointment—'ceptin fer it bein' in technicolor. The fireball jist done come and went, and there set Uncle Jerry's dump truck, good as ever, with the addition of a lazy torch-like flame a comin from that filler pipe and a nuther one from the previous described red and yeller gas can still jist a settin' there on the ground.

Instead of puttin' out them thar flames, which would seem like the logical priority, Bubba jist sat there tryin' to make heads or tails of the sitiation. Aside from Junior a laughin' and a stompin' on his head a couple a dozen times, it slowly dawned on Bubba—the brains of the operation—that it were that darn rascal what had done caused this unfortunate turn of events.

Next thang I knowed, both Bubba n' Junior were a' thrashin 'round in the dust tryin' to stuff their fists into each other's mouth, with only a smidgeon of success. Now, I were none too worried 'bout the outcome as I'd seen them two yahoos a clobberin' each other with rocks and big ol' sticks and ain't seen neither ever done much damage, not so's one could notice, anyways.

As fer me? Yeah, I was still there alright, but I'd done scooted myself up a step or two closer to the doorway. I weren't 'bout to get b'tween that mess o' fists and feet. And seems, I was either too dumb or havin' way too much fun a' watchin to get my li'l behind home like maybe I shoulda.

When the dust done settled, so to speak, and the last flamin' orifice had been extinguished by a double handful of dirt—which I am purdy sure had the effect of more than fire extinguishin' on Uncle Jerry's dump truck and, by extension, Uncle Jerry's employment prospects, I's a thinkin' that the above described fiasco would norm'ly warrant a cursory trip to the local emergency room fer Bubba. But 'tweren't like that at all.

Once't Bubba had kicked and punched Junior to his individual satisfaction, he done f'got his own tattered condition and—not even a botherin' to wipe his bloody nose—set right back to his 'riginal plan. In fact, it become evident that neither of them had been discouraged from their consid'rable hatred fer Davy and the sweetness of the divine possibility of watercraft ownership.

Follerin' the plan, Bubba, from somewheres in the rubble of all the trash that made up their yard, got hisself a dirty glass cider jug with a thumb loop. Them jugs was everywheres back then and mighty handy. And so it were, after all that fuss, the jug got filled part ways with gasoline and an old dirty rag got shoved down its neck. Seems all systems were now a "go."

Son, let me tell ya, it's a won'erful thang to have a plan that considers ev'ry possible contingency; and Bubba n' Junior, they had done figgered out such a plan! Iffen ya been a follerin' from the beginnin', ya already be a knowin' that this plan involved some ill-gotten gasoline, a glass jug, a dirty rag, matches, rocks, a shovel, and a yet to be identified burial site fer Little Davy. Mosta these thangs was carefully laid out at the river's edge with all the efficiency of a speedily contrived ambush—'ceptin fer the shovel, that is; cuz, after an unsuccessful search fer a gravedigger, they'd done decided that Davy's poor excuse fer an oar would hafta suffice.

That bein' the case, what was fixin' to happen is, to this day, a turn of events so unusual that it is etched forevermore on my memory in every possible detail. Here was Little Davy, a lone soul adrift on a lazy river, jist a follerin' his passion and purpose, tired from paddlin' upstream and then fin'lly lettin' go to drift with the natural currents of the river, all the fruits of his labor in one basket, and all the world 'round him jist a plottin' to own that particular river-goin' basket.

Chapter 5
Battle Royale

You'da thought Bubba was General Patton, firin' off orders to Junior and Junior snappin' to like a boot camp recruit. I all but expected the lad to salute, and by golly he did; a snappy, left-handed, badly executed version with his fingers in the Cub Scout salutin' position.

These boys were so dirty at this point that they did not need, in my opinion, camouflage of any sort to blend in with the muddy banks. However, Bubba did require Junior to apply an additional coat of mud to his face; and of course, bein' a good commander, he did likewise. Mind ya, the best mud fer this purpose was to be found at the mouth of their family's direct access to the river sewer outlet. Nice dark stuff. The only flaw with this camo paint was that the blow flies thought they'd done found themselves two walkin' turds.

Eyes trained on the western bend, jist a swattin' at the blowflies, Bubba n' Junior were fairly droolin' to execute their brilliant scheme. It was a gettin' toward noon, and they both figgered it was 'bout time fer Davy's return voyage with his valuable cargo of bloated animal cadavers.

Bubba n' Junior were 'specially scornful of Davy fer this particular practice. As one might could imagine, this were a highly contributin' factor to their disdain and their "rung or two above" mentality. It seemed to validate their plans to kill the lad, as they had decided anyone passin' his time doin' such a thang did not deserve to live 'longside upstandin' river rats like themselves.

I'm tellin' ya, it sho'nuff be amazin' what folk can justify once't they deem a body less human than themselves. Tis a sad sitiation fer sure. But, once't again, this old man has done taken to ramblin'.

As time and circumstance would dictate, here come Davy a driftin' with the current in the dead middle of the river, jist where them boys wanted 'im. They lay against the muddy banks, quiet as church mice, with their improvised bomb, a book of matches with two left, and a selection of rocks the size of goose eggs. In the distance, the noontime siren floated on the heavy, humid air. It was time fer lunch, but I wasn't goin' nowheres. Standin' a ways off, I was all eyes and just a huggin' myself a tree.

What happened next was like sumthin' straight out of a John Wayne movie. Davy keeps a comin' on the river current like a sittin' duck. He set low in the boat and the boat set low in the water. I figgered it was either carryin' quite the payload, or he jist done got behind with the bailin' can. His boat looked small and lonely in the middle of the river, and the air seemed to get thin and charged with an eerie type of electricity—which I learned later in life is purdy standard in an ambush of this magnitude.

As the little boat was about to come abreast of the boys, Junior, now an expert with matches, proceeded to light the danglin' rag on their homemade bomb. Both of them lettin' out war whoops, Bubba took the flamin' jug, wound up like an Olympian discus thrower, and let 'er fly. The jug hit the water 'bout five feet in front of Davy's boat and disappeared in a splash. Jist when I's a thinkin' that all had come to an anti-climactic end, that thang emerged still on fire and jist set to bobbin' along in the current.

Them boys commenced to throwin' their collection of well-chosen, goose-egg rocks at the glass jug attemptin' to create their much-anticipated explosion. However, when one or the other done hit the jug and shattered it, they only succeeded in creatin' a slow spreadin' fire across the surface of the water 'bout five feet in front of the boat; and there that fire remained, travelin' downstream at an identical rate of speed as Davy's payload.

Bubba n' Junior now stood agape on the shore, havin' seen their painfully devised plot fall victim to the natural elements of the river's current. Davy, on the other hand, seemed to have derived new life from the failed attack. Black smoke a rollin' in front of his boat, he suddenly let out a war whoop of his own and, to my astonishment, grabbed his shovel and commenced to rowin' like a bat outta hell straight toward a shocked Bubba n' Junior.

Once't he got up to—what I guess he considered to be—rammin' speed, he dropped his make-shift oar and knelt high and upright like Washington a crossin' the Delaware, his boat continuin' toward the south bank directly at a shocked enemy force, double in size, but standin' motionless like a pair of manikins sportin' the latest in blow flies.

Now folk, there has been many a Naval battle written up in the annals of history that do not compare with the events that were 'bout to foller. I had the privilege of bein' an eyewitness to these here happenin's, and I can tell ya that nothin' of this magnitude has crossed my path since. Not even whilst havin' survived my stint as a nightshift police patrolman, a Marine Corps Captain, an NIS Special Agent, and a bodyguard fer the rich and famous—the likes of which included many encounters with bad guys and shenanigans that have done slapped me with the most hinder parts of humanity and takin' me to the deepest dungeons of the depraved.

50

Son, I'm a comin' over to tell ya, from somewheres in his overloaded and makeshift watercraft, Davy produced a prized, mangy, bloated, gray cat deader'n the Third Reich. He knelt tall, holdin' the critter by the tail and, to the puzzlement of all present, began a swangin' it above his head in a circular motion like Roy Rogers fixin' to rope an outlaw. Bubba n' Junior was still standin' there like bronze-colored, fly-infested statues; and Davy were a comin' right at them a hollerin' an' a swangin' that critter 'round his head like a man possessed by a spirit of some bygone Biblical warrior. Prob'ly the same as what I imagine Samson might have looked like when he was a slayin' thousands with the jawbone of that ass he'd done come up with.

It was one of those moments in time when time itself done held its breath. It was like the air had been sucked out of the atmosphere, and the cruel realization of ultimate disaster seemed to dawn upon the hapless victims. Bits of glistenin' matter, no doubt consistin' of the cat's decomposin' innards, were a broadcastin' from its gapin' jaws under the power of centrifugal force.

Bubba 'n Junior's eyes met at that instant of knowin' that their carefully constructed plan had failed as bits of putrified matter began hittin' them and stickin' to their skin. By their reaction, you'da thought it was flamin' white phosphorous burnin' its way through flesh and sinew. Them would-be assassins and boat thieves turned tail and attempted to scramble up the bank, a slippin' and a slidin', losin' forward progress to gravity and the greasy mud, their eyes in blank stares of utter horror, and their mouths open in silent screams of agony.

Little Davy had found a way to turn his ripe acquisition into an efficient weapon of mass destruction. Like sand crabs tryin' to escape the attack of a ravenous seagull, Bubba n' Junior crawled up over the crest of the bank jist a gaggin' and a retchin' and a runnin' fer higher ground.

Yes indeedy.

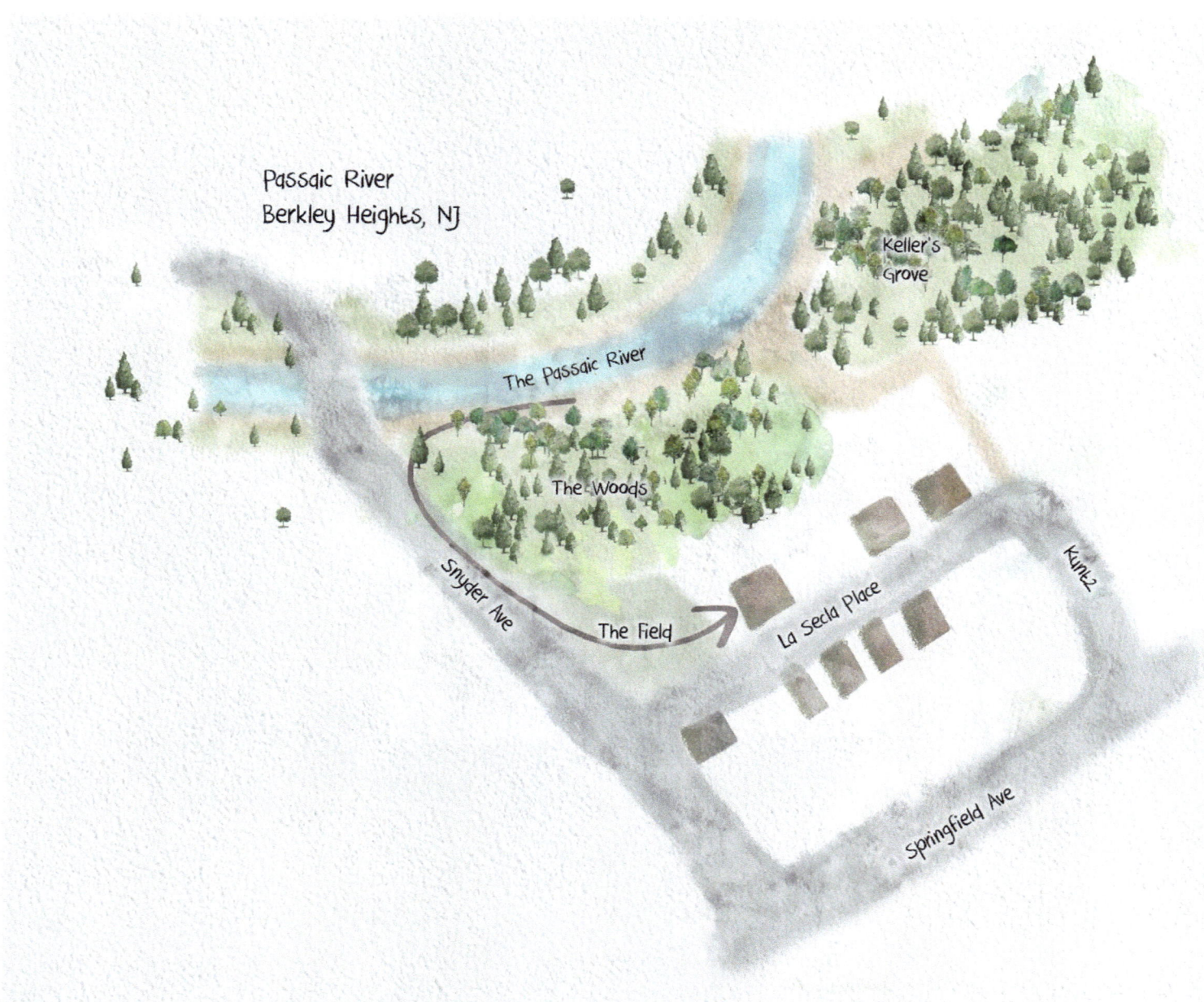

Passaic River
Berkley Heights, NJ

Keller's
Grove

The Passaic River

The Woods

Snyder Ave

The Field

La Secla Place

Kuntz

Springfield Ave

54

As Bubba n' Junior crawled up the banks, gaggin' and a wretchin' and madder n' all get out, I took off runnin' upstream… scared to death of what them hooligans might do next. I'd been a watchin' them two yahoos long enough to understand that they were mighty persistent in their evil intentions. One might even say, obsessed.

I ran all the way to Snyder Avenue bridge, climbed the muddy banks, and hurriedly made my way up Snyder Avenue and 'cross the corner field on La Secla Place. By the time I reached home, I was a changed lad.

Ya see, as tiny and diminutive as Davy was and as off-puttin' as his cadaver-collectin' practice were, that little whippersnapper was a boy of incredible ingenuity and imagination. But much more than that, he took what little he could scrounge up, added it to the *right down, rippin' radical, river rat resolve* inside of him, and came out victorious.

So, long b'fore I ever heared the Biblical story of David and Goliath, I had been an eyewitness to my own such historic event. Seein' Davy do what Davy did, why, it lit a fire and a knowin' in my gut that has stayed with me my entire life.

As one who was incessantly picked on by the neighborhood boys about my own scrawniness, I come away from that experience knowin' that I, little Dickie Dempsey, could be a Davy Hendrickson. I, too, had a passion and a mission; and I, too, could win against all odds.

From that day forward, if I wanted somethin', I went after it—no matter the size, the fear, or the number of roadblocks and pitfalls.

57

Epilogue
The Rest of the Story

I had just started the third grade when something caught my eye.

Oh man! Look at that! A store for rent—right on Springfield Avenue!

I took a moment to memorize the number on the sign, raced home, and picked up the phone.

"Number please," the operator requested, and I breathlessly recited the number. After a short pause in which I could hear my heart pounding, there was a click or two and then...

"Hello," came the female voice on the other end of the line.

Oh, thank goodness, it's a lady, I thought. *They're so much easier to talk to...*

"Hello, Ma'am. I wanna rent the store with the sign on Springfield Avenue." Confidence oozed from my little voice.

"Uhhh... what do you intend to do with the space?"

"I wanna open a store, Ma'am!" My excitement was obvious.

"Oh yeah? What kind of a store do you wanna open?"

"A detective store!" I gushed. By gosh and by golly, I could feel it. My dream was within reach!

"Hmmm," the lady's voice faltered, "How old are you, young man?"

"Why, I'm eight years old!" I answered proudly, never imagining this could be a problem.

"And to whom am I speaking?"

"This is Dickie Dempsey." My voice carried the obvious assumption that she would recognize my name and understand that I was, indeed, royalty.

"Well, Dickie Dempsey," the nice lady began, "I think you'd better talk to your parents about this detective store of yours and give me a call back."

Of course, I never called back, but this didn't stop me from dreaming. At the time, I was enamored with all things Dick Tracy. I wanted just one thing: to defend the weak and heroically solve crimes.

And now, after being a witness to the *right down, rippin' radical, river rat resolve* of Davy Hendrickson, I felt unstoppable.

The problem with my newly engaged bulldogged determination was that I was still physically weak and small in stature. Tenacity often requires more wisdom than it does strength and aggression. And in Davy's situation, that dead cat was what one might call "wisdom." Unfortunately, this was a lesson I had to learn the hard way.

My "detective store" phone call at the age of eight followed me into junior high. As fate would have it, that little storefront was owned by a family named Guidetti. The Guidetti's had two sons just ahead of me in school. During sixth grade, I attracted their attention when I tenaciously took on a boy named Jerry, probably the largest kid in the school. As I recall, the fight was over a seventh-grade girl and a very illogical crush I was nurturing. This hulk of an eighth grader thoroughly trounced my frail, 60-pound body; but because I refused to quit—despite the beating—it served the ill purpose of garnering the attention of the entire student body, including the Guidetti brothers.

So, in addition to making a name for myself by refusing to give up and foolishly getting my little behind kicked over a girl that wasn't the slightest bit interested in me (and whose name I can't recall), I was being teased about a phone call I'd made several years earlier. Things certainly do have a way of coming back around.

This story perfectly illustrates the dogged determination that was born in me that day on the muddy banks of the river. Against all odds, I was *right down, rippin' radical, river rat resolved* to push through my fears and past every seemingly insurmountable obstacle that presented itself. Not just insurmountable, but *bizarre,* freakish, unfair, and downright unbelievable. On the journey to fulfill my passion, I encountered false accusations, moments of stupidity, one injustice after another, a ton of *no's,* a series of rejections, and more roadblocks and pitfalls than I desire to recall—each one with the power to finish me off and end the pursuit of my dream. I had every legitimate reason to quit at each juncture along the way. However, in my darkest moments, my mind would replay Little Davy swinging a dead cat with that fierce look of determination while his enemies scattered, and that same fire would reignite in me.

Thank you, Davy Hendrickson.

Time after time, I had to pick myself up and find another way. Take a different path. Engineer a means to circumvent the roadblock. Scour around for my own dead cat. Approach it from a new perspective. Momentarily surrender to a detour while reconnoitering my options. **All the while gaining the knowledge, experience, and skills I was going to need to excel when I finally got to fulfill my passion and live my dream.** Ya'll hearing me?

As a Special Agent for the Naval Investigative Service, now known as NCIS or Naval Criminal Investigative Service, I was immediately deep selected for counter espionage (or spy chasing) and became the "go to" person for major crimes, such as arson and homicide. After four years, I was selected as Agent Afloat—a coveted, independent duty assignment as the only law enforcement officer aboard the USS Constellation, basically a city of five thousand adolescent Navy and Marine personnel. This assignment covered every spectrum of criminal activity including terrorism, narcotics, murder, assault, arson, and civil rights violations. Little Dickie Dempsey was the only "sheriff" in town, protecting the weak, heroically solving crimes, and bringing justice to the criminal element aboard the ship when deployed and stateside when docked.

Dream and mission fulfilled.

Right now, you might be feeling like your own journey has been just a series of one detour, roadblock, setback or disappointment after another. Like Little Davy, you may feel like you're on constant alert against an attack on your purpose and mission. You might even be afraid that you're about to walk into the worst ambush yet, complete with the equivalent of tripwires and claymores—or your very own Bubba n' Junior. I've been there **so** many times, and I feel compelled to tell you: **Do <u>not</u> take it personally.** It's just life's way of weeding out the uncommitted and undetermined. Those that can be talked out of their dream and their mission... will be.

In the face of disapproval, obstruction, or hostility, determine to embody the *right down, rippin' radical, river rat resolve* of Davy Hendrickson and choose to be unstoppable.

Whatever opposition you may be facing, I want you to know that, even at this moment, you have at your fingertips everything you need to overcome the obstacles that are before you. As meager as you may feel your assets are, all that is needed is for you to pick 'em up—you know, that stone for your sling shot, that jawbone of an ass, or that dream you think is deader'n the Third Reich. Pick it up with a hand empowered with passion, purpose, and a good dose of *right down, rippin' radical, river rat resolve.* Accompany that resolve with a loud, guttural, "Hooorah!" and prepare to enter into a realm of glorious victory, the likes of which you've never seen before.

It is yours for the taking.

I am both a witness and a testimony.

Carry on, Warrior.

About the Author

Richard "Dickie" Dempsey was born in Berkley Heights, New Jersey, in 1948 and grew up playing on the muddy banks of the Passaic. As a young lad, he discovered his gift for storytelling when his older brother would beg Dickie to tell him bedtime stories each night. As a father reading to his small children, he was known for embellishing the story by going off on tangents far beyond the plot line of the original author. As a grandfather, he made up ongoing tales about the Pop sisters: Lolly, Soda, and Tootsie. As a preacher, he was known for his storytelling... Biblical stories, stories of Bubba n' Junior, stories of his own tragedies and miracles, and stories of his escapades as a teacher, a cop, a Marine, a Special Agent, a private investigator, a bodyguard, and a builder.

This book was written to memorialize Dick's storytelling ability and to share the legacy message for which he'd like to be remembered: *Right Down, Rippin' Radical, River Rat Resolve*. This dogged determination is woven throughout the pages of his own story, and it is the one thing to which he attributes his many successes. To Dick, this is one of the most valuable assets he could leave his children, his children's children, and their children for generations to come.

"Sir Wonderful" to his wife of 37 years, Dick resides in Florida with Mandolin Rose (Mandy) his beloved emotional support companion; Theddee, his "Good Morning, Beautiful"; and Tre, his youngest son and fitness coach. He is a father of five: Dustin, Jennywren, Hannah, and Destiny, and Tre, and currently Umpa to seven: Haley-Rose, Chloé-Rose, Emily-Rose, Mia-Rose, Liam, Oliver, and California. His greatest joy is getting to spend time with his kids and grandkids.

As a disabled veteran, Dick is an active member of the Marine Corps League, a newly inducted member of the Military Order of the Devil Dogs (Florida Pack) and serves as chaplain for the Heart of Florida Detachment. He volunteers for the Polk County Sheriff Department as a citizen patrolman, and spends his days telling stories by painting pictures, his new-found love.

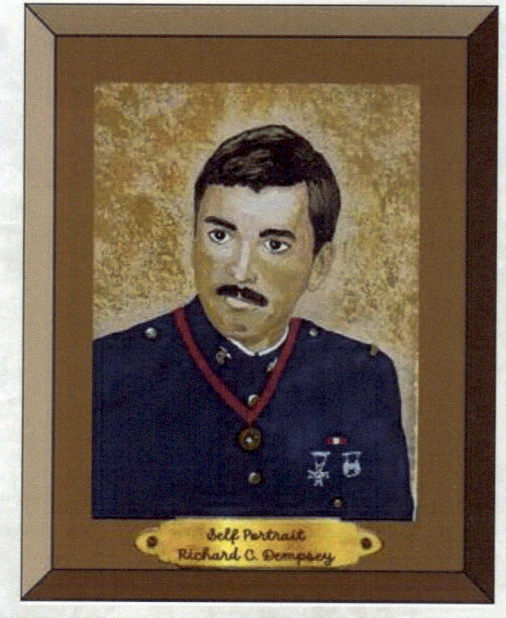

Self Portrait
Richard C. Dempsey

The River
Richard C. Dempsey

Mandelin Rose
Richard C. Dempsey

The Believer
Richard C. Dempsey

www.ingramcontent.com/pod-product-compliance
Lightning Source LLC
Chambersburg PA
CBHW040813120626
46547CB00004B/531